Spirit of Place

EARTH, WIND, SKY & WATER

The Poetry of Michael J. Leeb

ESCHIA
BOOKS

The Publisher: Sky Dancer Books is an imprint of Eschia Books Inc.
Website: www.eschiabooks.com

Library and Archives Canada Cataloguing in Publication
Leeb, Michael J., author
      Spirit of Place : earth, wind, sky, water / Michael J. Leeb.

Poems. Issued in print and electronic formats.
ISBN 978-1-926696-31-7 (paperback).—ISBN 978-1-926696-29-4
(pdf)

I. Title.

PS8623.E44385O55 2016   C811'.6   C2016-901948-9
                                             C2016-901949-7

Project Director: Dianne Meili
Editor: Dianne Meili
Layout & Design: Gregory Brown
Cover Design: Gregory Brown
Cover Image: Foreground and hoodoos: © bgsmith/Thinkstock;
magpie, © RCKeller/Thinkstock; background waves © CPD-Lab/
Thinkstock
Photo Credits: © FrankMcC/Thinkstock (p. 6); © Ideas_Studio/
Thinkstock (p. 92)

We acknowledge the support of the Canada Council for the Arts,
which last year invested $153 million to bring the arts to Canadians
throughout the country.

Nous remercions le Conseil des arts du Canada de son soutien. L'an
dernier, le Conseil a investi 153 millions de dollars pour mettre de
l'art dans la vie des Canadiennes et des Canadiens de tout le pays.

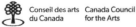

Conseil des arts   Canada Council
du Canada   for the Arts

Produced with the assistance of the Government of
Alberta, Alberta Media Fund.

PC: 29

List of Poems

BOOK II: The Syllabics or The Writings..........92
The Geography and Indigenous History of Little River Country

Book 1

The Magpie Asks…

for the generosity and solidarity of
Walter Henry Leeb

The Magpie Asks ...
the Cottonwood knows

the magpie asks
"where are you ... I know your voice"
I only smile
      (look)

a talkative magpie
now scolds me   for a mischievous trick
then   flies away

early morning calls
an ephemeral distance   seems far away
the magpie says

cottonwood poplar leaves
dancing   in the wind   sun   and   sky
uplift the spirit
      (soul)

near the water
the cottonwoods grow   stretch forth their roots
await the spring

ferns amidst stones
the hidden basalt   of an ancient seabed
leaves amidst change

beneath the branches
gazing upward   through sunlit leaves   and sky
the cottonwood knows

sky of crows
flights high above   amidst dark grey clouds
cold north winds

sky of gulls
soaring   in a windswept breeze   encircle above
a storm approaches

change of heart
the cottonwood's leaves   dance for joy
while looking   upwards

warmth of heart
leaves of cottonwoods   in full autumnal color
shine brightly about
          (forth)

the magpie sits
in silence   has left to fly away
know more heard
          (here)

A Raven's Song

a Raven's song
as prophetic criticism   of contemporary society
the guttural voice
and ominous demeanor
of One who lives
in two separate worlds   earth and sky
                           past and present

sits perched above
on a lamp standard

gives a homily | song
amidst rain and an overcast sky
lament and admonishment
for ways of the past
and things of the future

a dark grey omen
of things yet to pass

Two Ravens Share: A WindSong

fledgling flights
the incipient exercises
of a young raven
braking with wings
after having been carried
rapidly with an airstream
turns gradually
a slow about-face
with a cautious measured wariness
remaining stationary in flight   hovering
floating on snow mists and wind
holding wings slightly angular   downwards
into the strong gale
of a cold east wind
a mid morning snow storm
an approaching icy chill

she's joined now by another   her sibling
that seeks to emulate her
to share the same song
after stopping adjacent   parallel
and with an earnest look
similarly tests herself
turning, then performing
a WindSong   sung in silence

with the same adeptness and skill
taught by the gracefulness of Nature herself
until the two turn in unison
another about-face

holding their place in the sky   motionless
defying the wind's strength
if only temporarily
to sing in harmony
as kindred spirits   together

as they lift their wings level
slowly and in one accord
after having nodded in agreement
are carried away with the wind
on the silent wings of   a WindSong
that soars and floats together
knowingly with the wind

Aviary of the Sky

early in the morning
while watching the sky
two ravens soar past high
on another icy wind from the east
where the wind gathers the cold
by running across the frozen prairies

suddenly
another raven flies near
and makes a long gentle arc
over the studio
as if to watch me
he circles and returns
by soaring low and purposeful
in a curving arc
over the aviary
where i look upwards in wonder

is it his curiosity on seeing me in my aviary
or ... perhaps he sees a reflection of himself?

i watch ravens from the studio
an indoor aviary looking outwards
with an obverse perspective
and a differentiated view
through wall glass and ceiling
from the warmth and comfort of indoors

safe from the chill of winter outdoors
where ravens take flight
in the aviary of a sky
among passing clouds and winds
and the varied moods of nature

is this of interest to a raven ?

i watch ravens while I walk
along paths near the river
on warm sunny days
or sometimes when it's windy
and the sky is overcast and grey
where the disparate views of nature
no longer are separate
when I'm no longer in my aviary
of wall glass and ceiling
the artificiality of separation
from sky and earth
and instead have ventured out
into the aviary of ravens
that belongs to Nature and Creation
to seek
to learn
from them,
while in their aviary,
and the One who made us both

THE MAGPIE ASKS...

The Aerie

A treetop eagle's nest
toppled by a hailstorm
of strong gale force winds

the aerie of eaglets
cast in willows
now cast into
the creek

sits fallen toward its side
intact yet though
upon a rocky shoal
near the shallow water
beneath the cottonwood
the nest once sat upon
upheld by thick branches

untold eaglets
their numbers uncertain
now silenced
within their aerie
ravaged by the suddenness
of wind driven hail and rain

while adult eagles
soar high aloft

sombre dark forms
voicing their remorse
to a sad sun and sky

as clouds disperse
revealing the storm's wake
the inconsolable solace
of thick cottonwood branches

THE MAGPIE ASKS…

Voice of a Raven

alerted to a nearby voice
I look upwards
momentarily confused and diverted
by a wrought iron crow

then notice past the sign
two ravens in a cottonwood
the male's soothing voice, cooing softly
and the female's quiet deference

an unusual utterance
from the guttural, throaty calls
of throat singing ravens

they court each other's affection
on a bright and warm winter's day
after the heaviest snowfall of the season
the *Lenten* promise of renewal and spring

although still early
has initiated a courtship

the two rub each other's bills
held open widely
in the same manner
that ravens rub tree branches
a gesture
seemingly of friendship

except surprisingly
once or twice
the ravens
in mutual innocence and curiosity
gently touch each other's tongue
then rub beaks again

I divert my eyes
in modesty
to afford their privacy
with thoughts of spring
and a *Lenten* promise
from the voice of a raven

Canoe Journey

a paddle dips gently into shallow water
the journey begins
gliding along the water's surface
memories of the past emerge
shrouded in distant fog

I.
do crows migrate?

yeah … but ravens don't

they look the same to me

can't tell them apart

how many times has this question been asked?

II. ,
two young boys wrestle with each other
like two opposing thoughts
bear cubs dressed in buffalo robes
slapping each other in the face
until they laugh
 memories are that way sometimes
 searching for the opposite
 groping for the elusive
 like a paddle in water
 shrouded in distant fog

musing now with uncertainty
uncertain of the destination sought
an idea surfaces
perhaps his dodem is the bear?

**they walk that way … they're double jointed
that's how they climb trees**

i like the way they walk

perhaps his dodem is *Makwa*

a paddle dips gently
the journey …
gliding along … searching the shore
searching the past
shrouded in distant fog

silent waves lap at the bow
open water leads to
a narrow waterway through sedges
cattails billow in the wind
another elusive glimpse of an otter
while a swallowtail dances near the narrow

III.
a voice yells from the stern
lean into it
waves splash over the bow
water fills the canoe
i close my eyes

the Old Man plays his tricks
while we all enjoy a laugh

i no longer hear that voice from the stern
it has left like a merganser taking flight
the journey …
shrouded in distant fog

Canoe Journey II (At the Lake)

a merganser hen and young ones
four or five
sunning and preening
feathers and down
afloat atop a log
amidst cattails
and sedges

while the distant call of a loon
drifts across the lake
through a foggy distant mist
breaking the eerie stillness
of long shadows cast along the shore
lodge pole pine and spruce

i float my canoe
toward the mergansers
occasionally paddling
with silent cautious strokes
careful to observe the silence
of early morning lauds
over the bow

at first
mergansers feign indifference
at my presence
until at close proximity
the hen decides to swim
hastily she takes to leave
with little ones in tow
their downy wings a-flap
while they run along the surface
webbed feet all a-splash
breaking the eerie stillness
of long shadows cast along the shore
lodge pole pine and spruce

II.
over the bow
elusive glimpses of a muskrat
with furtive glances toward me
appearing unannounced
only to disappear just as hastily
among the cattails and sedges
breaking the early morning stillness
nature's observance of *matins & lauds*
a silent disposition
towards nature's own
a teleology of spirit
and natural environment

over the bow
the swallowtail dances
on a silent gentle breeze
careful to observe
the early morning lauds
the ontology of life

Backbone (Red Deer River)

I.

over the bow
swallows dip low
with grace and determination
skimming the surface
of slowly flowing currents
their homes along the mud-walled banks
little colonies of hermetic caves
or the earthen vessels of the Essenes

silence lingers
to be punctuated by intermittent riffles
that mildly disturb the silence
with staccato wavelets
that yet   must be negotiated
but only as momentary digressions
from a contemplative setting
of idyllic seclusion

even clouds that threaten rain
give way to sunny breaks
smooth   gentle   drifting
on glassine water

pelicans stand as sentinels though
in the shallows along the shoreline
or fly above in groups of three
directly above the canoe
as if warning of impending dangers
of water hazards best avoided
prescient in their presence

II.

first views now of the rapids ahead
serenity torn asunder
amidst a raging frothing chaos
water descending a rocky ledge

steep banks
no chance of a portage   too late
        velocity increases
             propelling forward

the canoe turns sharply sideways
by some unknown force
of wind gusts and water
dropping from the ledge

the backwater
presses the frame's side
hard against the backbone
a veritable weir
realizations suddenly apparent
visceral

and then
intuition guides the paddle
pushing free of a watery prison
only to
    capsize

stay with the canoe
intuition admonishes
swimming   with the canoe
this way then that
still gripping a paddle
    into

    deep

powerful

    commanding

waves

until a safe landing is possible
at last
along a muddy shore

then
    bailing   floating
                then finally
a return to paddling
and
        eventually

III.

    a continuation

but first
    a cold   rainy   night
    soggy clothes and sodden tent
    trembling legs ward off   *hypothermia*

a sleepless night brings an early morning
that leads toward
    other waters
    placid   soothing

between   foggy   mists
      spirits

the renewal of hope

Canoe Journey (A Memory Of)
(Red Deer River)

I.

a paddle dips gently
tenuous at first
into shallow water
as a journey begins

along sandy shoals and
small verdant isles
rocky shores
lined with cottonwoods

silence lingers
as the paddle languishes
in slow flowing waters
to be punctuated occasionally by
the scraping of gravel
in the shallows

a cloudless sky brings sunny warmth
and the lethargy
of old age
the listlessness of time

the canoe floats onward
in time and space
almost imperceptibly

swallows dip low
over the bow
exuding a tranquility
a monastic silence
the discernment of presence
the remembrance of the past and future
drift past and onward
with their attendant expectations

pelicans are notable
in their absence
boding well
for the moment

II.
first views now ahead
another water hazard
also best avoided
a Gethsemane of test and trial
Dominus flevit
with so many
how to choose the course
the avoidance of perdition
through

a rock garden
of
     vast   boulders   surfaces

not unlike numerous turtle shells
sunning themselves above the waterline
their segmented and spherical forms
luminescent
discernible from a distance
over the bow

THE MAGPIE ASKS...

velocity increases
        propelling forward
           too late

the bow is wedged
high-centered
while the stern
fills with water

a voice yells from the stern
to abandon the canoe
an allowance of time
to bail then float
and
        finally

           the dislodging

an allowance of time
for

       a continuation

but first

a swift re-entry
into the canoe
a necessity to be negotiated
with the reassurance of providence

the renewal of hope

Late Summer Lake

The distant calls of a Northern Loon
have an eerie echo
amidst the silence
of a mid morning fog
that lies low over the lake
in a misty grey silence
that suddenly is pierced
by the harsh sounds
of water being slapped by the wings
of a noisy pair of loons
seemingly alerted
to my presence

on approach to the shoreline
quite the opposite is apparent
and instead
a male loon gives chase after his mate
despite the lateness of the season
of a cold August morning

she thwarts all his efforts
time and again
by using her wings to accelerate
her abilities to outswim him
with short sudden bursts of wing beats
and adept dives underwater
whenever he nears too close
or seemingly catches her

chasing her the length of the lake
repeatedly and persistently
with purposeful intent and determination
despite all her efforts of avoidance and evasion
and uninhibited or constrained by my presence
both visibly nearing exhaustion
the drake still continues his chase
and only after her reluctant submission
until apparently succeeding
her mate then leaves
flying off towards the afternoon sun

then remarkably
two young females
Arctic Loons from the far north
appear from hiding along the shore
among sedges and grass
slowly approach
the exhausted loon
first one then another
with tenderness and concern
these young ones
preen and softly nuzzle the lonely female
childless of her own
to console her and comfort her
while their own mother loon
watches at a distance
then joins her own young ones
in their unspoken display of empathy and kindness

a return to the early morning calm
of fog
grey stillness
and a silent   late summer lake

Autumn in the Wind

with delicate swoops
and elegant dancing
autumn leaves in the wind
gently uplifting
then slowly descending
upon a silent   calm breeze

the butterfly awaits
unlike the autumn leaves
the silent reprieve
from the whims
of the autumn wind
to swoop and dance
its flight predetermined
by billows and breeze
til' along comes another
another reprieve
the silent calm
of the autumn breeze

and yet

are these mere whims
or flights of fancy?
of butterfly
of leaves
the vagaries of billows and breeze?

or instead

the willing of nature
a teleology
an order of things
the will of a silent breeze
of autumn in the wind

Mirror Lake, Alberta
(A Memory Of)

I.
drifting silently
with smooth paddle strokes
that make soft ripples
upon the glassy water

a solitary loon calls
at paddle length
across the lake
a trill of six notes
a measured decresçendo
a Pythagorean rhythm
an aliquot of harmony
a neo-Platonic form

the perfection of beauty

II.
dénouement

after fishing for pickerel

as sunset approaches   on a day canoeing

over a placid calm lake   a return to the shores

III.
fishing for pickerel
we caught mostly pike

then afterwards ...

gutting and de-heading
scaling and filleting

for

pan fried fish and roe
seared fresh in butter

The Voyageur

At paddle length
across the lake
a day's journey
toward new found land
and an unknown shore

une nouvelle esprit
un esprit de voyage/de découvrir/des temps
un esprit comme   L' Esprit

Arrow River

Straight and narrow
with swift flows
and deep pools
limestone monoliths within
large and smooth
eroded
and rocky ledges
of sharp-edged slide-stones
angular and narrow
form small chutes
water weirs
at low water
late in the seasons
or in years of drought
imperceptible
all
at high water
deceptive
undetected
when the Arrow flies fast

II.
A series of rapids
small chutes
visual entropies
amidst fluvial chaos
a narrowing
of the watercourse

the gentle sounds
of fast flowing water
unlike those
of riffles
that emanate
an auditory chaos
or a warning
of even faster shallows
and restless waters
further

near the crossing though
where the soft eddies
lap against the shore
of sharp stones
the riffles
are distant
and the rapids
forgotten
when the Arrow is in the quiver

III.

The sheen and shimmer of light
on the water's surface
ripples of soft stillness
deep water ripples
windswept by a gentle breeze
that makes transparent the water's depths
that reveals the soul
a rocky riverbed
of polished stones
and a grey overcast sky
threatens a storm

IV.

The soft patter of rain
now forms
concentric wavelets
radiating outwards
until the river's flow
dissolves their patterns
slowly
imperceptibly
the water flowing
onwards
towards another rapid
deliberate
with the intention
of nature's purpose
the resolve of a river
the water's way

V.

Along the river
a grotto
v-shaped   and pointed
inverted   ^   skyward
an arrowhead
irregular and jagged
carved in stone
by the river's strength
and
eroded
beneath
a dry shoal
with a single pole
thrust in sand

a spear shaft
a proprietary marker
within the grotto
along the river's edge
a sanctuary
refuge
from the thunder
rainstorms
and the winds

VI.

Past rapids and chutes
riffles and eddies
a change of passage
a widening of narrows
a flooding outwards
along the flats
beneath the mountain
and the talus slope
where beavers build lodges
and mudflats
near grassy shores
at water's edge
among the shallows
that form
the slender deep pools
of long willow lakes

VII.

Dippers singing sweet melodies
place their nests
on rocky ledges
hidden and undetected

an organic enclosure
an opening on its' side
for fledglings
yet to be born
clinging to an *arête*
of folded and steeply sloped
metamorphic limestone
above the river's edge
on a warm winter's morning

among a dozen denizens
that stay sheltered within
the warmth of nests
most often
buffeted by wind chills
on cold winter days

a lone dipper swims
in the shallows near shore
then dives beneath water
no longer visible
walking the river bottom
on spindly legs
or swimming below
defying the river's current
in search of larvae, or minnows

then re-emerges
to warm itself
amidst the sunshine
of refracted light
from a heavy, late winter snowfall

after two successive dives
it swims for shore
to join the others
among leafless cottonwoods
in a sing-song melody
of trills and whistles
the songs of a water thrush
the blackbird dipper
singing sweet airs
and odes for a springtime
the renewal of spring songs

VIII.

The arrowmaker
descends the slope
returns homeward
from an ancient site
a quarry
on a high ridge above
with sharp-edged stones
a lithic collection
of chert points
or trade goods

while below
the Arrow courses
in the flats
of the valley
the slight meanderings
in serpentine directions
form tributaries
though few

sedentary water
less deliberate
and lacking inertia
seemingly
still flows
imperceptibly
toward another narrowing
the Arrow on the string
straight and purposeful
taut and narrow
where water flows fast
and then the Falls
as the Arrow Maker passes by
with the winds

A Dipper's Nest

A small deep pool; at the bottom; of a two foot drop

Inwards
then dipping downwards
through a cold water trap
then inwards again and
upwards into
darkness
a cavernous space
within
a shell of stone
a black limestone monolith
a hollow dome
of the rock
or beaver lodge where
the nest hides
secure and dry
awaiting hatchlings and then
a baptism by water
before first flight

a dipper's nest
and the arrival of
nesting material
clasped tight
in the beak
twigs and moss
then sees
and with reluctance

a wary aversion
decides to dive
revealing its nest site
disappears again
within
inwards
to safe haven
shrouded in
a stillness of night
the dark night
of shell and stone

River Otter

early morning frivolity
awakens me from sleep
the sudden splashing of water
from a creek outside my tent
peering through an opening
of tent and willows

a river otter rolls
then dives
looking for a catch
of trout
or only minnows
as otter plays *solitaire*
an enjoyable game of   *go fish*
with an exuberance
and innocence

until he takes notice
a wild look of defiance
sputters through nostrils

then a look of remorse
after first   our surprise

                               a pair of *deuces*

now swims away   nonchalant

Upper and Lower Meanderings

The headwaters and confluence of the Arrow
(Crowsnest) River with Napi (the Old Man) River

Upper and Lower meanders
curvilinear sinuosity
the serpentine meanderings
of a river's flow depths

with a series of oxbows
both upper and lower
near headwaters and confluence
separates the distance of
surface water boundary

and *between*

eau de source and *fin de courrir*

a deep water lake fed
by aquifers and
flooded cave passages
into *Crowsnest (the Arrow)*
a fluvial network of
closed and flooded conduits with
an abundance of springs

karst water
running its course
towards the Falls   *Lundbreck*

near its meeting place with *Napi*   *The Old Man River*

2.

flying fast and straight
the *Arrow*
a river with a purpose
of intent
flying with deliberateness
towards the flats of the valley
where beaver lodges dwell
widening the narrows
of the watercourse
inhibiting the flow rate
into mudflats

along the *Turtle*
the *Arrow*
adjacent
the mountain slope
seeks swiftness

desires to
run a flight of fleetness
past a *mountain that moves*
that threatens to disrupt
this intention, this saliency:

the predetermined and
primordial meeting with *Napi*
and
the assurance of *longevity*
acquired through the endeavor of
a river's life essence

une raison d'être

3.
(beavers, too, have other ideas though)
yeah   they usually do:

the floodings of
shallow lakes
the slowing of flow rates and
the forming of oxbow channels
beyond
until

4.
at long last
the river resumes
in crests and waves
flights of earnestness

running to *Napi*
the primeval trickster
who also, has still yet,
further ideas

for a river that
plunges off
a hardened sandstone ledge

a tributary junction of
rimmed-in cliffs

the new beginnings
of an equilibrium
a compromise of nature

where swallows and dippers
dip and strike
lift and drop
against the water

and build their homes
at a convergence
together

Notes

Upper and Lower meanders are riverine names from the region of Ephe-sus (i.e. the Upper and Lower Meander River) mentioned in an article by: Dora P. Crouch. *Geology, Water, Antiquity*. OnSite Review. Calgary, AB. Issue #29. p. 5.

Terms of reference used for the scientific terminology on hydrogeology within this poem were taken from the doctoral dissertation of: Stephen Richard Hurst Worthington Karst Hydrogeology of the Canadian Rocky Mountains. McMaster University, Hamilton, ON. 1991. (paper 3542).

Napi is the Indigenous Niitsitapi (Blackfoot) name for Old Man, or Old Man Coyote (the trickster) and the Old Man River is a name in reference to Napi.

Arrow River is the Niitsitapi (Blackfoot) name for Crowsnest River; and The Mountain That Moves is the Indigenous name for Turtle Moun-tain, also the site of the 1903 Frank Landslide, Crowsnest Pass, Alberta, Canada.

A Winter's Day at the Old Man (A Memory of)

The young man fell into the Old Man
slipping on snow capped stones
amidst icy waters

How was the Old Man?

The river's still the same
He gave a rather chilly reception though

Is that possible?

What would Heraclitus say?

It's possible,
the young man's not the same
but the Old Man remains the same

something like that

that makes no sense to me

what? about the damn Dam?

that makes no sense to me either

River Water Drum

A hollow echo
intermittent and irregular
resonant deep water's
two-toned drumming
boom   *boom*

a deep water drum
like a heavy stone
thrown
a muted thud-splash
and quick-sink
distant   **near**
    the *same*

sounds of
deep water pools
and tawny ice

what is that sound?
is that your drum?

the deeply resonant sounds of
stretched rawhide
and sudden thermal changes

at early Spring break
and thaw
a brackish river's
drum song

Lyons Creek

water on ice, and ice over water, from rain on snow;
the lair of Mishepishu, the underwater lion of the Anishna'abe

Water rushing over ice
clear water on opaque thickness
a creek yearning to be a river
or
a creek yearning only for the river

running wildly in torrents
after a rain-on-snow event
a freezing rainstorm
on floating clouds of mist and fog
the appearance of *Mishepishu*

sudden in its consequences
followed by a warming thaw

further downstream
the late winter runoff
like brackish tea water
spilling from a culvert
the effluent of an industrial site

    gushes yellow
        a sulphurous brown effluent, a copper sulphate yellow
            water from ironstone
                flowing over a ghostly sheen
                    of thick ice
                        towards a melt pond of deep water

                Mishepishu in hiding
                    hidden beneath the opaque
                        in a deep water lair

Thick Ice in mid-Winter

glaciation
and crystalline forms
the thick frost
of condensation
and opaque ice
obscuring windows
and mountain views

a wind chill
from the frozen prairies
towards the east
rushes through the valley
across an ice field
in the early mid-winter morning
until the warmth
of a mid-day sun
melts away
these glaciated panels
of frosted glass
and thick Holocene ice

a *diorama* of change

A Thick Ice Melt

In a *Greenland* of blue ice
and grey sky
with snow fog and haze
lies an ancient ice field
of molten ice flows
and glacial melt water
a coastal ice shelf
of undulating melt flows
from upwellings
with snowy white ice ridges
that collapse and implode
then sink below
into the melt water
of ice flows beneath
rapid fluvial development
along a *moulin*
the making of a new sea
a chasm rift with icebergs
afloat upon an ice current

the warming of thick ice

A Sighting

a sighting
a tautology
expressed within
itself
connotes an acknowledgement
of exclusivity
an elusiveness of nature
that once
was sighted
of surly demeanor
and solitary recluse
best left alone

a wolverine

Spring Moult

spring moult of a ewe yearling
nesting material for a magpie
the silent chatterer
collects the soft moult

both ewe and magpie
in calm indifference
she sits atop the ewe's shoulders
gently tugging the moult free
as the ewe grazes on dry grass
exposed by the warm Chinook winds
the sunny morning
of a snow drifted meadow

she then ingests it
the lanolin and wool
easily swallowed
used later for the lining
a nest yet to be built
in a tall sturdy poplar

and collects tufts of hair
some windswept away
then caught in tall grass
that she diligently gathers

a new spring's nest

Five Poems/Two Crows

The crows return
resume plaintiff cries
amidst summer rains

Outside my window
the crows sound mournful
feels like autumn

Crows think to migrate
yet it's still mid-summer
autumn fast approaching?

Crows make plans now
to make a journey
autumn soon gathers

A gathering of crows
curiously silent
foreshadows
winter's long absence

An Unfortunate Crow

A crow __ distraught
encircled by blackbirds
fends off his rivals
half-heartedly

pesky young cowbirds
enjoying the game
pull at some tail feathers
smile in delight

a stalemate ensues

the crow now calls out
a pleading lament
in supplication
to sun __ sky

then suddenly with stealth
hidden by pines
another arrives

swooping in low
scatters the blackbirds
saving her mate

not first without though…

the angry scolding of
young, pesky blackbirds
that delight in misfortune

Nature's Days & Works (Lyons Creek)

High afternoon sun
glistens on flowing water
a kaleidoscope of light
on shallows
with rays of light gleaning through
the shadows of
dense cottonwoods and
poplar pollen
drifting on water and
the gentle breeze of
a heat wave
a dry wind in
the intensity of sunlight
the *theogony*
of Nature's
days and works

II.
The cottonwood knows…
abides
the passage of time
from season to season
and from each season
from deeply rooted being
the teleology
of its essence
from the pollen of
wisdom

Notes
A reference made to the poetry of Hesiod, *Theogony. Works and Days.*
Morrissey, C.S. (translated by) Hesiod. *Theogony. Works and Days.*
Talonbooks. Vancouver, BC 2012.

The Darners (A Memory of Lake Pend Oreille, Idaho)

those darn Darners
yeah, they're difficult to identify

the ones we sighted at Sandpoint were a yellow-green
probably a Variable, green form

darn it, that's what I thought

the Darners were moulting
after forming in the water's depths
emerging from a larval state
pale and colorless
clinging to the dock
by the multitudes

with emergent wings
between water and sky
the warmth of a glaring afternoon sun
brought to life from a dormancy
in cold lake water

chartreuse green dragonflies
by the multitudes
that whirred and hovered in flight
awaiting still others
or skimming the water's surface
in search of prey
born of water and sky

The Darner of Jura

From the screen of the vehicle
a Darner
with translucent wings
rescued intact
held cautiously by the forewings
despite the sticky residue
of veined planates

a specimen of beauty
so much so, as to be
not collected

a buffalo fur-trimmed thorax
of long rusty brown hair

a sky blue spotted abdomen
forming a segmented tail

her dark green blue eyes
intense watery pools
intent and defiant

her abdomen convulsing
with laboured breathing
she tried to regain her balance
with frantic efforts
to make a flight of escape

she sustained a wobbly balance
atop a large stone
where I set her
hoping for her recovery
her wings regaining their rhythm
although slowly
her breathing more regular
as she perched horizontal
an awkward orientation
for a Lake Darner
or more probable
a sub-Arctic species
having assisted her
I left for Jura   not certain or knowing of her fate

II.
My thoughts wandered as distractions
along the road

self doubts about a Darner

and the cryptic voice of the night before
an enigma in the darkness
that warned of Jura:
I think you'll see my evil sister

nevertheless
arriving at the trailhead
after a distance of
perhaps 2 kilometres

astonishment and joy
soon found solace
at the sight of a Darner
flying
and at a remarkable speed

the rescued Darner
had followed
and with a smile and a nod
we set off for Jura

along a grassy trail
a deeply rutted track
then a widened dry stone creek
until finally
the mouth, a portal
to the slot canyon of Jura

III.
Along the bottom of the canyon
a faded pictograph
of ghostly white figures
limbless
in a linear formation
illuminated
by refracted light off water
that dances low on the panel
a small curvilinear grotto
of dancing figures in light

high sculpted serpentine walls
of chalk white ikaite mudstone
an ancient flood channel
the slot canyon path
past the curvilinear opening
an interstitial narrow

until a blockade of
skinned poles with syllabic script
etched indecipherable   although familiar
Nakoda

form a barricade
an obstruction to further passage
with a carved Mountain Goat's head
atop a shaft pole
as a silent sentinel
or guardian spirit
and just beyond
a thick pole
a skinned pole hazard
placed across a deep pool
necessitating caution

the creek then widens
with a seep
along a sloped east wall
and a monolithic masse
of a higher curved wall
on the west
a gravel creek bed
with a trickle of water
late in the summer

enamored by the site
the darner asserts herself
by hover-guarding my further progress
until a moment of understanding

she indicates her desire to leave
having guided me along the way
without a conscious awareness

she hurries northward now
on her migratory flight
after a melancholy farewell
of mutual thanksgiving

IV.

past smoothed basalt boulders
surface covered with snowflake patterns
of crystallized salt on dark basalt stone
like frost flowers of sea salt

saline water flows gently
across saline stone

and a forested opening to the west
with a sodden, grassless footpath
adjacent to a campsite
sheltered beneath fir trees
with three circular stone fire pits
and a few lodge poles   pines

a hastily abandoned camp
strewn with long metal roasting forks

in the creek bed
the figure of a loggerhead turtle
fragmented, severed, and cast in stone
with other fragmented creatures
scattered along the creek
apocryphal and eerie
an ancient cataclysm

V.
Retracing the course of the creek
and returning to the canyon
stopping short of it's portal
another discovery

that of an *evil sister*
and the memory of a cryptic voice

the visage in stone
of a menacing sneer
and furrowed brow
looking southward
in threat and defiance
challenging all who would dare enter

a foreboding of the apocryphal
and an ancient cataclysm
all that lies beyond
along the Jura

Impervious

the Seven Sisters
seven stone monoliths
vertical
in a semi-circular apex
resembles Stonehenge
 a Neo-lithic structure
formed though
by alpine glaciation
the scouring of ice
passing through
stands as sentinels
adjacent to a horn
an *Ararat*
the Crowsnest
a "nest" above ice
"unscathed" by the Pleistocene
nevertheless
rounded and sloped
with glacial till
and steeply sided slopes
glaciation
passed around and beneath
its "nest" of stone

and further

Turtle Mountain
another horn
that held aloft its peaks
among clouds and sky

yet below
its shell of stone
fractured by ice
with deep fissures
eroded instead
from within
by the seasonal cycle
of   freeze   thaw
with a sudden storm
toppled a peak
an historic landslide

fragility and impermanence

impermanence of the seemingly impermeable

the slow and sometimes sudden
morphology of the impervious

Swimming Concretions (ca. 8000 BC)

Jellyfish
bulbous
with uniformity of size and shape
lack tentacles
are inverted
and striated with layers
the porous membranes
once filled
with sediment
from the turbidity
of a massive flooding
an inland sea
shallow
and an estuary
inundated
suddenly
with floodwater
during the pluvial era of
The Deluge
and an alti-thermal of
distant ash clouds
are now
swimming concretions

but what would Solon say?
Critias grasps for an answer

a Socratic dialogue left
(ca. 380 BC)
indeterminate; unfinished
the lithic remnants of
an ancient cataclysm
the flood of Noah

Poem (Untitled)

time and space
lack certainty

sands gently swept over dunes
an ephemeral passing/
an empty expanse/
an infinite horizon/
an unending sky
of moon and stars

a liminal determinism as impossibility
existential as thought

The Bergsturz

a poem based on the Landslide at Frank, Alberta, Canada.
(Turtle Mountain) April 29, 1903.

Gravity
having kinetic potential
alone   awaits

an early morning Spring
of unseasonable rains/
the disparity of temperatures/
an icy thaw among fissures/
and the cold air inversion
of a gale force wind.

An early morning storm
unknown to most
with a town asleep below
and "The Mountain that Moves" above
now sets into motion

a landslide

of epic proportions.

Dust and boulders, slide rocks and mud
That slip across the flats
of the river valley below.

A mud slip that slides   across marsh and meadow
                    and runs down the slope,
                              then across
                         the valley beneath.

Velocity
having destructive capacity
alone   won't await ^

              "the Mountain that Moves"
              and a storm set in motion
              All over/
a mere single moment.

              Limestone boulders   of varying mass,
           a phantasm of featuress   a not distant past.
                 The loosely bound mudstone,
                       an amorphous mass;
              the conglomerate of pebbles, gravel, and silt;
              a textural beauty of deep ochre color.

                    Geomorphology;
                 a metaphor for change
                    of bounded stone
                    at the perimeter.

           now only   perhaps

                 a lithic memorial
                 amidst the tragedy
                 of a not distant past.

See the geological report of: McConnell, R.G. & Brock, R.W. *Report on the Great
Landslide at Frank, Alta.*, 1903. Edmonton Geological Society.
Edmonton, Alberta. 2003.
"The Mountain that Moves" is the name historically used among indigenous peoples
for Turtle Mountain.

Lime City
(near Hillcrest Mines, Alberta) ca. 1920

(Lime City ceased the production of lime at this site in 1923)

tower *draw kilns*
with semi-circular arches
and slight entablatures
for structural support
at the tower's base
resemble the towers
of cathedral architecture
Romanesque
or crusader fortifications
watchtowers
of smoothed, thick walled, cyclopean stonework

now
the abandoned battlements
of economic progress

lime from limestone
placed in wooden barrels
made on-site
for an emergent economy
the westward expansion
of a new *Dominion*
of railways, coke ovens, and kilns

watchtowers
of a former era
the incipient development
of industrial monoliths

the lithic ruins
of siege engines

once called: *progress*
now, a modern aesthetic
the perception of beauty

found   in   ruination

Obsolescence

Structural obsolescence
abandoned interventions
Industrial
the functional anomalies
of a forgotten era
Lost in the forgotten silence
of utilitarian inadequacy

narrow islands
of slender poplars

intersperse the river's flow

are parallel
to adjacent rock gardens

the rounded stones
of concrete pilings

and the mixed fill
of cement supports

the buttress and forms
of trestles and bridges

made transverse
in silent defiance
against nature's obstacles

now crumble and erode
in structural obsolescence
freestanding in the river
the abandoned reclamation
of nature's primeval forces

A Train Forgotten

The clanging of bells
and blasts of the horn
intermittent yet
impending
punctuates the silence and
announces the arrival of

a train

the proximate approach
of an auditory chaos
captivates attention and
the imagination with

the harsh metal sounds of
hammers on anvils
and the sharpening of blades

wheels on rails
of creosote-soaked
trusses

the rhythmic dissonance
of heavy rail cars

until its passage
through the valley

with muted horn blasts
hauntingly re-echoing

in the distance
a passing apparition

leaves as quickly as
it arrives

is *remembered* and
forgotten in
the returning

of stillness and
the wind

.

Kêyam

Kayas
Long ago
the buffalo were without number
the prairies were open skies
freedom without fences

the sun has set on those days

when yes meant yes
against the untruth of society

long ago never happens anymore

there is only
kêyam

a lament for the past
a fondness for the old ways
the *overgrown paths of the buffalo*

instead
long winters of hardship
and summers of drought

long ago never happens anymore

there is only
kêyam

a lament for the past
uncertainty in the present
an indifference for the future

leads to
pervasive distrust

there is only
kêyam
spoken too often

Notes

A poem and thoughts on contemporary society and indigenous culture
inspired by the journals of Edward Ahenakew and the stories of Ahena-
kew's grandfather: Chief Thunderchild; from *Voices of the Plains Cree*.
McClellan & Stewart. Toronto, Ontario. 1973.

The Cree word *kêyam* has many meanings that convey the idea of
indifference or "I don't care", when the true intention is one of serious
concern for a problem(s) within society.

"against the untruth of society" is a phrase used in part from a title of
a work by Eric Voegelin on *Hesiod's Poetic "Truth" Against the Untruth
of Society*. An excerpt appears in the notes of Morrissey, C.S. (translated
by) Hesiod. *Theogony. Works and Days*. Talonbooks. Vancouver, BC 2012.

Longing and Expectation

solitary

alone

loneliness

except

soliloquies

or

rarely

discourse

a glass of wine poured out
yet not consumed

a presence in absence

an expectation

a longing

yet   unfulfilled

waiting   in anticipation

insular   in hopefulness

as if withdrawn within a womb
a solitary room
sheltered from without
from *being*
within

in lonely expectation

Floating Lotus Pond

Dr. Sun Yat-Sen Garden (Vancouver, BC)

I.
Floating lotus pond
with golden lily pads
reveals a lotus flower

Its gentle petals
awaken
opens from within
toward the sunlight

II.
A painted turtle
motionless
stares and squints an eye

among curious
wide-eyed *koi*
gracefully swimming
motionless

III.
Another turtle
sits in solitude
squints an eye
knowingly

suddenly scrambles off
a stone perch
shuns attentive looks
disappears into the depths

IV.

The magpie sits now
in quiet solitude
atop a pine branch

as evening descends
awaiting the moonlight
of silent reflection

V.

Koi swim by moonlight
awaiting the daylight
of morning blossoms

Ode to Basho

A cool sip
after splashing water _
robins bathing

II.
scruffy feathered magpie
cries a lament
a flooding downpour

harbinger of omens
perched atop a newsstand
the magpie

portent of news
in black and white
the magpie

sopping wet plumage
feathers all askew
another downpour

The Sunflower and the Warbler

I.

Early morning warmth of sun
admires a tall sunflower
turning towards the sunlight

An orange tabby cat
suns and stretches
in the early morning light

II.

Flower petal wings
gentle flutters and swoops
a butterfly on the breeze

III.

Late summer morning
sipping cold coffee
feeling rather lazy

Late summer passes
beneath a cool blue   azure sky
autumn soon arrives

IV.

Thick poplar leaves
verdant green soon yellow
as the warbler

Golden yellow plumage
soon the leaves of autumn
when the warbler leaves

V.

Yellow fallen leaves
race on crystalline streams
rushing toward autumn

Sudden gusts of wind
swirl and turn
bringing a rainstorm

dark thick clouds
then sunny breaks
of iridescent green and yellow

VI.

i have seen the wind
dancing in the rain
tossing leaves in autumn

Wind driven rain
twists and swirls
dancing in the wind

VII.

Sparrows fly in the distance
like windswept leaves
in aimless twists and turns

Et. al.

I.
Hidden magpie calls
Amidst thick cottonwood boughs
that reach toward each other

II.
A brief paddling of wings
the magpie glides along low
swimming in air

III.
A magpie visits
outside my window
talking about autumn

Amidst the barren boughs
sits a magpie
complaining about the weather

Outside my window
a magpie sits
listening to the wind

IV.
Weeping birch boughs sway
lace fringes and bustle leaves
dancing in the wind

V.

Barren poplar boughs sway
with the voice of a magpie
chattering in the wind

The Honeybee(s)

I.

A golden honeybee
hums a sad song
near to my ear

II.

A honeybee struggles indoors
near the watery abyss of
a sinkhole
until set free
upon a dandelion

III.

Orange blossoms with clusters of petals
the colored hue of bumblebees

A begonia blooms the radiant rays of
sunshine
the abundant nectar of golden honey

Winds of Winter

Swirling gusts of wind
send snow from the rooftops
snow plumes of smoke

Snowflakes glisten in the wind
swirling dervishes of snow
dance in mid-winter sunlight

white-robed clouds
swirl and gently sway
with the winds of winter

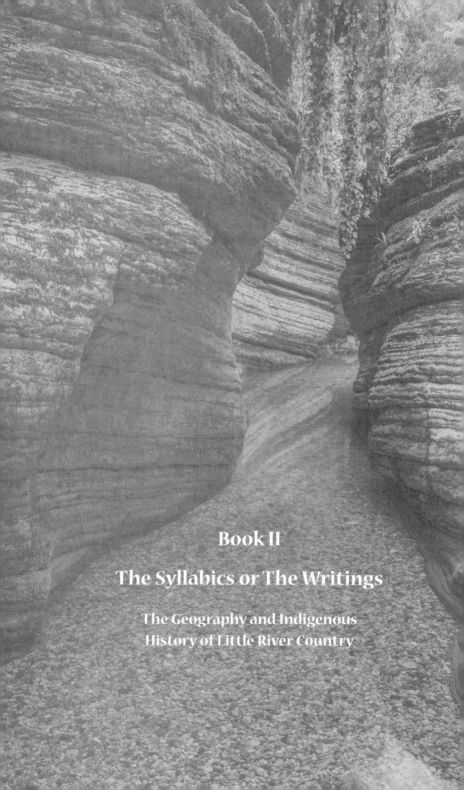

Book II

The Syllabics or The Writings

The Geography and Indigenous History of Little River Country

Dedication

**For the Memory of my father
Joseph Martin Leeb**

Little River Country

Little River or *Kin-nax-is-sa-ta* (*Niitsitapi* Blackfoot)
The River that Scolds (all Others) (Hidatsa)
Milk River (Lewis and Clark Expedition)

Little River
was not such
a little river
It flowed
both ways

i.e. has flowed both ways:
< < < from east to west (meltwater) (from Glacial Lake
Agassiz)
and currently
> > > from west to east

Little River
not (formerly) part of
the Saskatchewan River basin
an ice-free corridor
for at least the past 55,000 years
(Lethbridge/Medicine Hat southern limit of the
Laurentide ice sheet)[1]

During the *Paleolithic*
water scoured (66 *m* deep and 500 *m* wide)
a valley
the shoreline of
an ancient sea[2]

---

1   Barry, P.S. *Mystical Themes in Milk River Rock Art.* The University of
    Alberta Press. Edmonton, AB. 1991. p. 12

2   ibid p. 12.

where the Little River
now flows
within

chalky white (the Milk)
the rock flour from limestone and
kaolin in clay
upstream in
the Rockies

rock wrens burst from
hiding in shrubbery
along the baseline of
sandstone cliffs
while yellow larkspur sing
from sandstone walls
orange with iron ore
concretions

Fresno Dam
(on the Milk River, Montana)

"Captain Mike"
the guide at
the fort
caught a walleye (36")
a catch and release
while fishing at
the reservoir near
the damn Fresno Dam
a catch limit of 5

elevated levels of
arsenic and other
heavy metals in
the river
occurring naturally
at least supposedly

This reservoir
effectively diminishes
the river's vigour and
creates a lifeless spirit

an anemic river
without the
slightest riffle

a regulated, unnatural thing
more a canal
than a living river

heavily silted and
stagnant
with a thick muddy layer
on bottom gravel.

Phrases in italics taken from: Rees, Tony. *Hope's Last Home, Travels in Milk River Country.* Johnson Gorman Publishers. Red Deer, AB. 1995.

"Captain Mike" the Whiskey Runner
(at Fort Benton, Montana)

A taste of
Whiskey (190 proof) Everclear
with Jamaican spices and
a braided plug of
tobacco
molasses too
smoothes the *firewater*

all homemade
in a little oak cask
atop the counter in
the trading post

a one ounce shot
offered in
a tin cup
just like a Whiskey Runner('s)
moonshine (200 proof)
only a 2 proof more
I'd say
in 4 gallon tins though

Nez Perce battlefield (Bear Paw)
(September 30, 1877 – October 5, 1877)

South of the Medicine Line (Montana)

An exodus
the 1,170 mile journey from Oregon
an escape from mistreatment and
persecution
the result of bounties
placed upon the heads of
Nez Perce Indians
sought after by
wolfers that alleged
they were stealing horses
committing murders upon settlers
most probably though
mere allegations

they left with the intent of
joining the Lakota Sioux and
Chief Sitting Bull near Ft. Walsh

skirmishes and occasional battles occurred
along the way (Big Hole)
until the Bear Paw
hemmed into
the Snake Creek coulee
where a campsite was established
after a buffalo hunt

adverse weather conditions of
wind and snow
shortly after their arrival
at Snake Creek
a tributary of Milk River

~ 100 warriors | 400 U.S. soldiers/cavalry
        vs.
+ 50 Crow and Cheyenne scouts
and 5 days of battles

an artillery barrage
probably decisive in
the defeat of the Nez Perce
their encampment with non-combatants
the elderly, women and children
bombarded indiscriminately
after an ill-fated charge of
cavalry
the *irregular topography of*
Snake Creek *blunted* [3]
that first charge

the Nez Perce attempted to
establish a perimeter
with rifle pits and
a rocky outcrop
along the ridge of
the coulee

---

3   Rees, Tony. *Hope's Last Home. Travels in Milk River Country.* Johnson
    Gorman Publishers. Red Deer, AB. 1995. p. 228.

away from the encampment
eventually ineffective against
artillery and
US sharpshooters (snipers)

Snake Creek with
thick brush
choked with willows and
box elders
a slow moving rather stagnant creek
with many small oxbows
amidst wavy hillocks and
sharp wedged coulees
especially towards the south
the Bear Paw mountains
visible with their peaks
shrouded by snow fog and clouds
from bitter east winds

An oak tree marks
the ridge where
the Hotchkiss gun emplacement was
prepared to the south of
the tipi encampment

The "Hotchkiss"
a mountain rifle (1.65")
with rifling for
increased accuracy
an artillery rifle wheel-mounted

The larger "Napoleon" gun
(a Civil War era brass gun)
was used against the enemy
a greater distance
directly west of the encampment
Crow and Cheyenne warriors
stole the Nez Percé horses
during the onset
of hostilities

Soft loam hillsides
steeply sloped
with a tight serpentine course
provided a topography that
afforded earthen hollows
pits and
subterranean passages
as defensible positions
entrenched along
the small coulees
used by the Nez Percé

Starving and suffering with
the inclement weather from
a prolonged siege
a truce is arranged
Chief Joseph (Thunder Rolling in the Mountains)
makes a statement
of surrender:

**From where the sun now stands, I will fight no more,
forever**

thereby ending
the Indigenous horse culture of
the Great Plains
with the symbolic gesture of
handing back his rifle

Small memorials and gifts
are placed at stone cairns
where chiefs and warriors fell

the Nez Perce battle
near Little River country
only 40 miles from
the Medicine Line
safe haven and refuge

only the earth remains   forever [4]

---

4   The book of Ecclesiastes.

Red Rock Valley[5] (Alberta)

Size (estimate of diameter)	Whole	Sheared	Fragmented	Non-inverted	Conjoined
Large < 2 *m*	IX	V	V	II	I + I
Medium ‖ > 2 *m* | < 1.25 *m* ‖	IV	II	III		
Small > 1.25 *m*	III		XV	I	

Sample of area at Red Rock Coulee (near former estuary)

I.

A preponderance of
Sea nettles
a bulbous orange
jellyfish
lithic remnants of
a sea under stress
strewn about like shards of
clay/pottery

while others remain
wholly intact and
inverted
or sheared and
partially fragmented
their tentacles shattered
brittle and weathered
strewn adjacent or beneath
the remains of
an ancient inland sea

---

5   The more appropriate name of Red Rock Valley since it applies to a much
large geographical region/area than that of Red Rock Coulee. This name was
appropriated from a discussion with Dr. Hestor Jiskoot who made this
reference. (Dept. of Geography, University of Lethbridge).

II.

A catastrophic disbursement
extending 25 km west of
Writing-On-Stone and
east toward Bulls Head
the massive flooding of
an estuary of
a remnant saline lake
belonging to the Cretaceous yet
present still
in the Pleistocene
during an outburst flood
the southern outlet of
Glacial Lake Agassiz
(the South Saskatchewan River basin)
ca. 8000 BCE

III.

A torrent of rain
shapes a landscape
molded by water
an estuary inundated with
a watery slurry of
sediment
A paleoflood spillway of
Glacial Lake Agassiz (an estimate of ca. 9900 BP or 7900 BCE)

Rapid glacial melting
during an alto-thermal
the result of
distant ash clouds of
pumice
from the volcanic eruption of
Mount Terra (of Santorini)
coterminous

its elevated flow levels
for several months;
~ 700 years before
the waters began receding

a flood event like no other
the ancient flood of
Noah

IV.
A flood that caused
narrow jagged wounds
serpentine
in hardened sandstone and
steep-walled meanders
with wide swathes
through softer Cretaceous
sands and clays

Bentonite: volcanic ash clay
is also ubiquitous
having chemical properties
altered by saline water
the marine environment
dating from the Cretaceous from
airborne ash
landing on
and absorbed
by saline water

V.

Whiskey Gap and Lonely Valley
most likely the outburst floodways
where the eastward flood along
the Milk River ridge (Little River)
was breached
the cutbanks here
are among the highest

VI.

Sweetgrass Arch: a drainage system
from the Cypress Hills
to the Sweetgrass Hills (Sweet Pine Hills)
formed by the enormous effects
of glacial meltwater
an unglaciated area
not traversed by
the Laurentide Ice Sheet
forming the southern perimeter of
a saline lake

VII.

Pah-kah-kee Lake or
UnLucky Water (Pakowki Lake)
clear water with a foul odor
saline ? most probably
the remnant lake of
a Cretaceous inland sea
has no outlet

with evidence of oyster reefs (1 *m* deep)
melded or cemented together
it continues to decline in size
a shallow and highly alkaline
water
a false oasis
"discovered" by explorers
stagnant and undrinkable
shimmering
ephemerally
in a desert plain (within the Palliser Triangle)
the vestigial remains of
a paleo-sea

VII.
Early explorers of the 18th century had hoped for an inland sea.
A sea that would have an outlet to the Pacific.

VIII.
A lone Sea nettle
along an elevated ridge
near del Bonita
would suggest the furthest limit
of the Paleolithic
saline lake and
the only Sea nettle
to have managed to swim
to these easternmost limits
along the Milk River ridge
suffered the same demise

of an ill-fated swim
as those
at Red Rock coulee
inverted
of the same shape and form
overturned by
an act of nature and
the hand of
the Creator

The Writings
(Writing-On-Stone, Alberta)

A spirit place of
discovery
a discovery of one-self and
the discovery of spirit

imbued with the spirituality of
a cosmic order
an order of nature
providing a spiritual insight/wisdom
induced by deprivation (hunger and thirst)
a vulnerability
hence danger
an aridity

a place between
the celestial and
physical worlds
where transport from
one state to another
of being
is made possible

|| (physical) and (metaphysical) ||

with an intercessor
a celestial creature
providing insight, an
"allusion to flight" [6]

the flight of
the Thunderbird

requires
reconciliation for
cosmic unity
peace

II.
The capstones of
hoodoos
like drum rounds
are sometimes
inscribed/etched or
painted
and beneath
deeply scoured by
water (not glacial ice)
are thin and figurative
in shape
irregular
having an individuality

Hoodoos and
capstones
similar to
the outstretched wings of
a Thunderbird
or possibly
the shell of a turtle

---

6   Barry, P.S. *Mystical Themes in Milk River Rock Art*. The University of Alberta
Press. Edmonton, AB. 1991. p.59.

possess a hidden language
infused with imagery
become a source of
inspiration/imagination

III.
Hoodoos with detached
wing-like forms and
with x-shaped torsos
replicate
Thunderbird as
a celestial bird/spirit
headlessness
the "onset of invisibility"
the emergence of
the metaphysical with

lightening rods as
drumsticks and
thunder
the pounding of capstones

a trance struck
by a thunderbolt
and the struggle of
cosmic duality

**(Thunderbird/Skyworld and the Underwater
PantherLion/ Underworld)**

having layers of
meaning
as symbols of
survival and
individuality

IV.

Hoodoos having an incomplete
or abbreviated form/shape
are often featureless (almost)
having anthropomorphic shapes
only partially revealed
revealing an underlying reality
a spiritual reality of mystical meaning
definitive of experience
the spiritual searching of
the soul
for unrevealed forms or
interior truths
by inference
the transferral of ambiguity
to spiritual certainty
through spiritual experience
or perhaps
a conceptual process
the intuition of
possibilities and
the probable

V.

This place has
no written language (historically)
only rather
symbols as metaphors
or abstractions

Petroglyphs as
further expressions

an expression of spirituality or
narrative imagery
through geomorphology

a syntax
repeated in symbols
that are ideograms
having an abstract relationship
to its meaning
imbued with spirit
the spirit of
place

VI.
Rock art:
a form of communication
with spiritual beings/deities
made possible by
the writings in
figurative form/anthropomorphs
a mystical thematic language
discerned as
 icons of power
narratives of glory

The Syllabics of Place

An excoriated landscape
by wind
dusty and drought-ridden
having an aridity of soul
beckoning the solitary
seeking a vision

A sacred space
Not without
dangers
a land of shamans that
listen to the land
water and wind
crying for a vision
with vivid dreaming

The land
as a visual context
a "world" where
stones talk and
represent spirit being(s) and
 syllabics of place (topography)
provide a reference to
the womb-like presence
of Mother Earth

Little River Land

Rolling
hummocky
till plain
rough and
steeply gullied
badlands

A flat glacial lake-bed
terrain
deeply incised
meltwater coulees and
channels with the
clefts and fissures of
sheer-walled cutbanks

Varves (Writing-on-Stone, Alberta)

I.

Magmatic

Greatest Number of	27	< 43 (1) ;	< 80 (1)
Total Counted	9		
Thickest Layer at Base of Formation		~ 6 – 8 cm	
Thinnest Layer at Upper Portion of Formation		> 1.25 cm	

Sandstone (Hoodoos)   Site #3

Greatest Number of	< 27	(fewest [16])	
Total Counted	11		
Thickest Layer at Base of Formation		~ > 2.5 *cm*	
Thinnest Layer at Upper Portion of Formation		> 1.25 *cm*	

II.

Varves
watery syllabics
layers of evaporation
developed over
extended time
the drying up of
a water basin (lakebed)
leaving sedimentary layers
of varying thickness and
number

Occasionally magmatic
with pumice or
volcanic ash
imbued within sandstone
or fused upon
outer layers
airborne ash
upon saline water
absorbed
then settles
resting afterwards
upon the watery depths

from the volcanic eruptions
of the Mazama (5677 BCE)[7]
centuries after
the paleoflood or
the *Deluge*
in the time of
Noah

---

7   The Mount Mazama eruption of about 7627 years ago, just after the
paleoflood event during the time of Noah about 8000 BCE or 10,000
years ago.

A Watery Narrative

Varves
tell a story
a watery narrative
with a rippling effect
from ages past of
a slow transition from
lake to river

of a "world" or
landscape viewed and
understood in anatomical form(s)[8]
toponyms having a familiarity
as an act of memory
for the recognition of
a geophysical event
like the scales of a serpent
the moulting of
time

---

8   Yellowhorn, Eldon. in Brink, Jack W. and Dormaar, Johan F. (Ed. by)
    Archeology in Alberta. A View From the New Millennium. Archeological
    Society of Alberta. Medicine Hat, AB. 2003. p. 324.

Coffin Bridge (Milk River, Alberta)

At the distal end of
a gravel road
a bridge
its' name and origins (unknown)
demarcates a boundary/threshold of
a river
an ending and
new beginning
as evidenced by
adjacent rock art
(2 panels) biographic
on a sheer-walled embankment
convey a message/meaning of
ambiguity
phonetic symbols or
figurative drawings
where distance and proximity
form an alignment/perspective or
an orientation with
figurative forms
the analysis of land and landmarks
like clefts and fissures on
a riverine cutbank

NWMP OutPost
(Writing-On-Stone, Alberta)

Along the Little River

Near a former NWMP post
on the southern banks
adjacent to a coulee
is a traditional river crossing and
a traditional tipi campsite
within the sacred landscape

a wide-mouthed coulee
perpendicular to the river
splayed like the tail feathers of
the mythical Thunderbird
having a gradual descent
from the distant Sweet Pine Hills
the ridgeline as
an overarching wingspan
and a coulee lined by rocky outcrops
flared at jagged angles
like a rough-legged hawk

an expansive wingspan
forming the topography
the mystical shape of
the Thunderbird
descending
like a hidden metaphor
hidden within the landscape
a geosyllabic symbol of
a primordial past

II.

The Blackfoot would camp
across the river
on its south shore
near the NWMP outpost
where a coulee leads
directly to the Sweet Pine Hills
to the south

Biographic panels
were etched
of warrior records
invariably facing towards
the south
across the Little River
the orientation of
panels towards
the south
demarcating a boundary
Niitsitapi traditional territory
the *writings* as
as overt messages
and warnings
having a linear orientation
the same as
the erosive forces
of water
directed towards
enemies
from the South
Shoshone and
possibly Crow and Sioux

Little River hence
similar to
a battle river or
"fight" river
with enemy transgressors
that crossed the river
considered an act of
aggression

the exchange of
taunts and insults
across the river
that formed
a linear political alignment

with Shoshone "writings"
on the north shore
indicative of
an act or statement
similar to
"counting coup"

III.
Syllabics
most often Siouan (Writing-On-Stone)
and occasionally
Cree
although more prevalent
at Verdigris Coulee
situated further west
yet still

contingent
within
the landscape
as socio-political landmarks/language
a political border = a topographic boundary
with sandstone ramparts and
spyholes

Within a tapered cylinder
a small sandstone aperture
faces south
ensures
the defense of
territorial integrity and
the political configuration
of hoodoos and
sandstone cliffs

The Wounding of Horses
(Bear Paw Battlefield, Montana)

It is salient
a question
posed by a stranger
along the trail
one to be pondered:

whether Indigenous warriors
from various tribes
intended to dismount
US cavalry or
warriors of opposing tribes
by shooting at their mounts
were horses targets?   or
was this predominantly done
inadvertently?
an inadvertent part of battle?

some ledger drawings and
buffalo robes
depict wounded horses
though
since horses were sought after
and stolen
symbolic of strength
and pragmatic of purpose
it is unlikely
that horses were intentionally
or strategically
wounded in battle

though
not so
for mules
that had no part in
Indigenous horse culture

Buffalo and the Sun

Buffalo migration
was circular from
the "gathering place"
in the foothills
where they left
to winter
on the northern plains
to the summer calving grounds
of the southern plain
circular in the same direction
of the sun (clockwise)
the same direction
buffalo would run
in a pound

always with
the sun

Slow Flow of a Little River

The slow flow of
Little River
south of the Medicine Line
a wide valley
in the midst of sagebrush and
the parched
treeless prairie
except for
the tree-lined shores
of cottonwoods
that send out
their roots
by restful waters

Murphy's Pub (Havre, Montana)

Good Medicine ale
good for what ails
an Indigenous ale or
craft beer

served by
a young Native woman
by the pint
a full pint
of medicine and
a friendly smile

Lily Blossoms (Fort Benton, Montana)

I picked a sprig of
blossoms
with white
thread-like flowers

A *mop* of
iridescent threads
with entwined
woody stems
an *unruly climber* [9]
growing like an ivy
or clematis

at the far end of
the footbridge
the same "ivy"
as at Writing-on-Stone
near a gated entrance
to the river:

the taller heiress of
swamp-loving blossoms
an ancient sea lily [10]

9   Bain, John; Flanagan, June & Kuijt, Job. *Common Coulee Plants of
    Southern Alberta*. University of Lethbridge. (digital library; website)
    Lethbridge, AB. 2014. p. 32.

10 Keiran, Monique. *Reading the Rocks. A Biography of Ancient Alberta*.
    Red Deer Press. Calgary, AB. 2003. p. 49.

Sweet Pine Hills
(Sweet Grass Hills, Montana)

Intermodal transit
glimpses of
the Sweet Grass Hills
through double-decker railcars

The peaks of these buttes
visible with
low-lying fog
obscuring their forms
below

II.

The Sweet Pine Hills
a place of
spiritual refuge
represents also a place
where
the struggle or
battle
between good and evil
took place during creation
a place of
abundance
of buffalo
since the bison
first emerged from
a cave site
in the Sweet Pine Hills

III.

The south view
of west butte (Sweet Pine Hills)
has the appearance of
an amphibian
similar to
the fossils of
Red Rock Coulee

East butte
appears as
a water monster or
a creature with
several dorsal fins

Gold butte has
a pyramidal shape
that of a sea turtle
with very elongated
and splayed
frontal fins

A pyramidal head
a form
very similar to
the grotto
on Crowsnest River (Arrow River)

Both east and west butte
face the rising
and setting sun
in opposite directions
like revelatory bookends
and both
having a similar form:
serpentine
like water monsters
superimposed upon
the prairie landscape
symmetrical with
the middle butte (Gold Butte)

A pyramidal form
at the centre
forming a divide
between the primordial forces
of nature and
the polar opposites of
Good vs. evil
The Creator vs. chaos

Water Monster
(Writing-on-Stone, Alberta)

A water dragon; an ancient serpent as of old

Sculpted in sandstone
by the erosive forces of
water and wind
a Water Monster
along a narrow shelf
a ledge
curved slightly inwards
gently concave

A series of
dorsal fins
forms a ridge and
a wide gaping jaw
faces eastward
as if scolding
the impending flood
Awaiting atop
a high rocky outcrop
the highest vantage
in sinister earnest
buffeted by
gusts of wind

II.
A small cloud
flutters past the ledge
then falls dreamily

like a single leaf
tossed beneath the precipice
while a Painted Skimmer
or Meadowhawk
defies gravity
by hovering and
landing on the ledge

Deftly alighting again
then disappears to
where the sounds of
cicadas below
amidst silver poplar
willows and sage
float on a breeze
past a silent river
that scolds
(all others)

Milk River Skies

The Milk River valley
with long vistas and
remnant uplands
hummocky and
expansive
under the vaulted arch
of a prairie sky

only the distant
yelping of coyotes
enters the silence
of an evening
sky
intent on
twilight

Mass Extinction

The Pleistocene bison
migrated across
the isthmus
of Beringia
some 14,000 years ago
concurrent with
a glacial retreat[11]
then suffered
a mass extinction (ca. 8000 BCE)
cause unknown

although speculatively
the result of
a massive flood
during the pluvial era

---

11 Dormaar, Johan F. *The Alberta Stretch of the Milk River and the Mystique of its Surrounding Landscape*. Lethbridge Historical Society. Lethbridge, AB. 2010. p. 20.

The Atlatl

Innovation and change among Indigenous peoples of the Little River region

An innovation for
hunting
the atlatl
pre-dating the
bow and arrow
used as a type of sling
for projectile darts
with impressive ability
able to pierce rawhide shields
the atlatl
first used by the Crow
in the southern regions of
Alberta
in battle against the *Niitsitapi*

the Crow had the best horses

after the introduction
of horses (*elk dogs*)
on the northern plains
by the Shoshone (ca. 1730 CE)

although
the Comanche
first fought
the *conquistadors*
using atlatls that
penetrated
plate armor[12]

---

12 Historical accounts made by an Indigenous interpretive guide
(Pikanni) at Writing-on-Stone on August 27, 2014.

Blood Ochre
(Writing-on-Stone, Alberta)

Within
a desert varnish
on a sheer walled
sandstone panel
a smoothed sheen
is a borehole
an iron ore disc
amidst a grey blue sea
fused mollusks of
oysters

An orange eye of
a serpent or
the rounded sphere of
a Thunderbird's head
slate blue
with outstretched wings
is discernable

An anthropomorph
adjacent to
the blood ochre
markings of
several *coups*
gouged deep in
the sandy
granular walls
then painted
an ochre red

Blood-Clot Boy
(Kutyitosis: West Butte of the Sweet Pine Hills, Montana)

According to Niitsitapi *(Blackfoot) culture; a legend*
apparent from a northern view/perspective
of the Sweet Pine Hills

The reclining *Kutyitosis* (Blood-Clot-Boy)
in mortuary repose
lay himself down (west butte)
after his battle of
earthly life
witnessed the reemergence of
the bison from a cave
of the Sweet Pine Hills
after their disappearance
from the northern plains
long ago
in an ancient time
only to re-witness
the eventual
overhunting and
second final demise of
the buffalo

Songs of the Past

In the land of
an ancient sea
live the diverse
tribes and nations of
buffalo people

the buffalo now
long gone
only *the earth remains*
forever
as a phonetic voice
wistful and longing
singing of the past

Chokecherries

Goose down on willow branches
cling to red stems
snared by the wind
after goslings
take to water

In late summer
the webbed tents
woven by caterpillars
on small sun-sweetened
cherry boughs
pitted and dark
dry and shrivel

The blackened cherries
ripe and juicy
parch the throat
spitting out stones

The Bear Paw Sea

Named after the Bear Paw Mountains (Wolf Mountains)
of Montana

Unlucky Water
the remnant lake of
the Bear Paw Sea
a Cretaceous body of
water

An amphibian
and a juvenile
swim the shallows of
a delta
while salmon
swim nearby
eluding sea nettles

suddenly
the turbidity of
a rushing torrent
floods and fills
the delta

asphyxiating in
its totality
immortalizing in
its effect
rendered in
stone

II.

Sandstone columns
a place of
transition
from seafloor to
river bottom
with capstones
the deposits of
deltas and tidal flats
the retreat of
the Bear Paw

III.

A Sea of silence
that resonates upon
the landscape
unlike silent syllables
that emerge from nothing
their origin in
unknown words

The syllabics of
geography
like phonetic symbols
are pronounced
by the wind
and enunciated
by the rain
that shape and form
the language of
land
written in stone
long ago

Sated by Rain

A river sated
by spring rains and flooding
once a river
primeval
that scolded
all others
expansive in girth
swollen by rain
sated by an act of
deluge
an admonishment
a voice spoken
to a prophet
with a message of
judgment

II.

The receding waters of
an inland sea
made for
a dry and weary land

like a deer that thirsts
for running waters[13]

The aridity of thirst
within a landscape
is only sated by
rain

---

13 Psalm 42

Glacial Lake Agassiz
(Origin of an Ancient Flood)

From the unglaciated
southern outlet of
an expansive lake
a series of *cuestas* emerged[14]

long and narrow
extending westward
to the foothills
watery arms
reaching outward
umbilically
towards a floodplain
to a delta or
estuary

destined in time to form
an alluvial deposit
at the headlands
of an arid prairie
replete at its' southern limits with
sandstone
deposits arranged
as anthropomorphs
with the sudden birth pains
of a tidal flood

---

14 The Red Deer and Saskatchewan rivers were re-entrant rivers to Glacial
   Lake Agassiz. It is quite probable that smaller cuestas were evident in the
   area of Red Rock Valley. (see Elson, John A. in: Mayer-Oakes, William J.
   (ed. by) *Life, Land and Water*. University of Manitoba Press. Winnipeg,
   Manitoba. 1967. p. 40.

capstone hoodoos
along the coulee of
a serpentine
muddy clay bottomed
river valley

II.
A vast expanse
of water

receding slowly …
some 4,500 years
from its' furthest limits
reaching to *Unlucky Water*
at end moraines
the Porcupine Hills
and the Sweetgrass arch

only to evolve into
the aridity of

yellow-brown
silty clay

III.
From the vast and mysterious
a sea of
calamity and woe
a new beginning
an act of
re-creation

Conveyance (Writing-on-Stone)

A small dust devil
at my feet
a vortex of
swirling wind
as a spirit presence

proceeds a
hot and dry duster
a sandy
wind-blown landscape
in a spirit filled place

ghostly apparitions in
an ancestral commune
seek to convey
a message
shrouded

Rattler (Writing-on-Stone)

Along a sandy footpath
concealed within
a pit
hidden from view
a small   juvenile
rattler
sans rattle
lies in venomous ambush
awaiting hapless prey
makes its presence known
by peering above
when I sign a "hello"

elicits a scowl:

you don't have to
talk to the snake

Taking A Gander (Writing-on-Stone)

A gander
atop a capstone
with a banded face
masquerades as
Janus
looking forwards
while glancing
backward
at a river
that has flowed
both ways
searching the past
watching the future
of a setting sun
in transition

An Ancient Drowning
(The Palliser Triangle)

A catastrophic dispersion
the turbidity of sediment
from the Deluge   <Deluge in italics>
causes
widespread drowning
the flooding of an estuary
cements a moment
in time
thickened and veiled
afterwards
into hardened kaolin
and soft layers of
bentonite

A mass extinction
of sea creatures
the water monsters of
an entropy as antithesis
a time-lapse
fossilized
near the
subsurface
after a pluvial dominated climate
and the alto-thermal of
a rapid glacial melting
the withering of Agassiz
lapses into
a synthesis

of re-creation
evident in clay sand and silt
within the triangular aridity
of the Palliser

II.
Hope in desolation
trust after tribulation

from the depths of
the watery abyss

emerged

a new world
an expansive valley
as a grassy plain

with a river coulee
that witnessed
the genesis of this
re-creation
a new birth from
destructive waters

A river
that admonished
ancestors
and instructs
all those
in the present
that sings of remorse
an ancient song:

The Little River

The Land: Indigenous

Little River of
Red Rock valley

a land
Indigenous
as a corollary of
self identity

a place of
authenticity
of will and purpose
both in and of
the land
where the two
become one

A Land Sought

Lying in
languid supplication
a watery expanse of
flooded earth
until
a gradual reclamation of
land from
the waters

sought by land
a raven returns with

the baptismal promise of
rebirth
a land recreated and
a new covenant:

Never again shall there be
such a flood

As Long As

A hot dry wind
under
a warm sun
rushes along
as long as
the Little River
shall run

THE SYLLABICS OR THE WRITINGS

Immersive Language

Water
as immersive as
language or
a flooded landscape of
hieroglyphics
written in stone
etched in
the hardened sand
from an ancient flooding

as long ago as
yesterday

 as ephemeral as
desert rain

Notes

Words in parenthesis for place names are the Indigenous names for geographical features or locations, and immediately follow the common place names. These Indigenous names are usually those of the *Niitsitapi* (Blackfoot) (Kainai) people. Other Indigenous names from other Indigenous groups or tribes are sometimes given in italics, often within parentheses.

Short phrases or words in *italics* are most often words quoted from other sources with these sources noted in the footnotes. At times though, phrases in *italics* represent a person or a *voice*.

Acknowledgements

I would like to extend my thanks for the support
I received from the Canada Council for the Arts in
the form of a project grant (Aboriginal Writing).
Thanks also to Dianne Meili of Eschia Books and its
imprint Sky Dancer Books for all of her assistance and
comments during the editing process and for allowing
me the opportunity to share these poems with all of
you. A special thank you to Stephanie White, the edi-
tor of On|Site Review, for her several years of ongoing
support of my writing and for previously publishing
some of the poems in this volume; as well as to Stewart
Donovan the editor of *The Nashwaak Review.* Heartfelt
thanks also to my friends in the Crowsnest Pass for
your friendship, encouragement and generosity....many
blessings to all of you.

About the Author

MICHAEL J. LEEB, of Anishnaabe and German descent, is not only a poet but also a visual artist and fine art photographer who makes his home in the Crowsnest Pass area of southwestern Alberta. The land and nature are the inspiration for his work, and his poetry conveys his deep appreciation for the world around him and how it came to be the way it is. As he approaches a fissure in a rock, he contemplates how water and time may have done their work to create it, and commits the process to poetry.

Michael has honed his writing craft in residencies at the Banff Centre and in Blairmore. His prints and photographs are displayed in the permanent collections of the Alberta Foundation for the Arts, University of Alberta, Medalta Potteries Museum and Ino-cho Paper Museum (Japan).